Little BIG Chats

I0164191

My Safety Network

by Jayneen Sanders

illustrated by Cherie Zamazing

My Safety Network
Educate2Empower Publishing an imprint of
UpLoad Publishing Pty Ltd
Victoria Australia
www.upload.com.au

First published in 2021

Written by Jayneen Sanders
Illustrations by Cherie Zamazing

Jayneen Sanders asserts her right to be identified as the author of this work.
Cherie Zamazing asserts her right to be identified as the illustrator of this work.

Designed by Stephanie Spartels, Studio Spartels

ISBN: 9781761160240 (hbk) 9781761160103 (pbk)

A catalogue record for this
book is available from the
National Library of Australia

Disclaimer: The information in this book is advice only, written by the author based on
her advocacy in this area, and her experience working with children as a classroom teacher
and mother. The information is not meant to be a substitute for professional advice. If you
are concerned about a child's behavior seek professional help.

Using Little BIG Chats

The *Little BIG Chats* series has been written to assist parents, caregivers and educators to have open and age-appropriate conversations with young children around crucial, and yet at times, 'tough' topics. And what better way than using children's picture books! Some pages will have questions for your child to interact with and discuss. Feel free to use these questions and the Discussion Questions provided on page 19 of this book to help you assist your child with the topic being explored. Stop at any time to unpack the text together; and try to follow your child's lead wherever that conversation may take you! So, please, get comfy and start some empowering 'chats' around some BIG topics with your child.

The Body Safety titles should ideally be read in the following order:
Consent, *My Safety Network*, *My Early Warning Signs*,
Private Parts are Private, and *Secrets and Surprises*.
The remaining titles can be read in any order.

Meet the Little BIG Chats KIDS

Theodore

Asha

Ardie

Tom

Jun

Jamie

Belle

Lisa

Maisy

Tilly

Maya

Ben

Hi! I'm Maya.
Today we're learning
about a Safety Network.

I have a Safety Network.

These are 3 to 5
grown-ups who I trust.

I get to choose who is
on my Safety Network.

Mother

My Safety Network

Mr Sandos
(My teacher)

Grandpa

Auntie Carla

WHAT DO YOU THINK 'TRUST' MEANS?

7

If I feel worried, scared or unsafe,
I can tell a grown-up on my
Safety Network how I am feeling
and why I might feel that way.

WHEN HAVE YOU FELT WORRIED? SCARED? UNSAFE?

The grown-ups on my
Safety Network will
listen to me.

And they will
believe me.

There is more than one grown-up on my Safety Network.

If I can't find one grown-up on my Safety Network, I can tell another.

My Safety Network will be different to your Safety Network.

One person on your Safety Network should not be in your family.

Auntie Jo

Mother

Mrs Blink
(my neighbor)

Auntie Sally

Dad

15

Handprint drawing labels:
- Mr Sandos
- Auntie Carla
- Grandpa
- Mother
- My Safety Network

My Safety Network is very important to me.

And I am very important to them.

They are the people I trust.

Who is on your
Safety Network?

My
Safety
Network

DISCUSSION QUESTIONS
for Parents, Caregivers and Educators

The following Discussion Questions are intended as a guide, and can be used to initiate open, age-appropriate and empowering conversations with your child.

This book introduces your child to the idea of a Safety Network. At the end of the reading, help your child choose (and it must be their choice) 3 to 5 adults they trust to go on their Safety Network.

Page 5
Introduce Maya. Ask, 'What do you think a "Safety Network" might be?' Note: if your child is not familiar with this term, point out that they will learn all about a Safety Network in this book.

Pages 6-7
Introduce the term 'Safety Network' with your child. Discuss the term 'trust' and provide some examples of the actions of a 'trusted' grown-up, i.e. they make you feel safe, someone who listens to you and always believes you, a person who looks out for you no matter what. Discuss Maya's Safety Network. Point out that Maya chose these people herself. Ask, 'Why do you think Maya chose these grown-ups to be on her Safety Network?'

Pages 8-9
Ask, 'What do you think happened to Maya to make her feel unsafe? Who did she tell? Is this person on her Safety Network? Who would you tell if you felt unsafe?'

Pages 10-11
Ask, 'How is Maya feeling now she has told her mother?'

Pages 12-13
Point out that sometimes we can't always find a grown-up on our Safety Network and that is why we choose at least 3 people. Ask, 'Maya feels unsafe (worried or scared), so who is she telling about it? Is this person on her Safety Network? What might have made her feel unsafe?'

Pages 14-15
Point out that everyone has a different Safety Network; and that it's always the child's choice. Note: at least one person on your child's Safety Network should be outside the family, for example, a teacher, a family friend or a neighbor. Your child must feel safe and comfortable with that person and it must be someone you trust also.

Pages 16-17
Reinforce that the grown-ups on your child's Safety Network are people they trust and who care for them.

Page 18
Now is a good time to outline your child's hand and write the names of the grown-ups your child has chosen. Your child could draw a small picture of each person's face on each digit. Note: older children will benefit from having a phone number written also. Some children like to include pets or toys. These can be drawn on the palm. Point out that in an unsafe situation only a trusted grown-up will be truly able to help. As the adult leading this conversation, reach out to the people your child has chosen and gain their consent; pointing out that they should be honoured to have been chosen. Ensure they are readily accessible to your child.

For more books that include a Safety Network and Body Safety Skills, see Jayneen Sanders' children's books 'No Means No!'; 'My Body! What I Say Goes!'; 'Let's Talk About Body Boundaries, Consent and Respect'; 'ABC of Body Safety and Consent' and 'Some Secrets Should Never Be Kept'.

Little BIG chats

A series of 12 little books to help kids unpack BIG topics

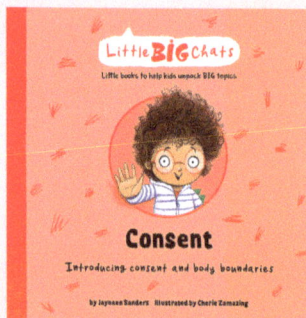

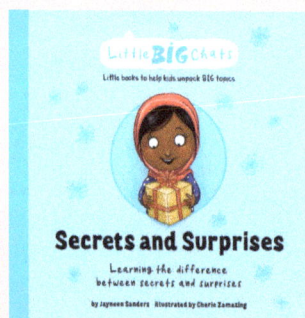

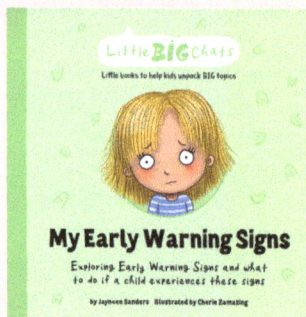

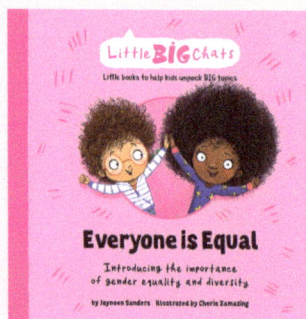

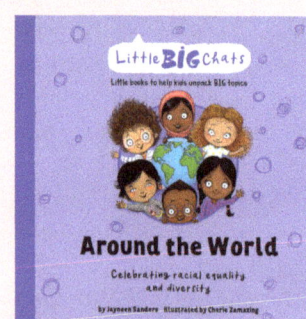

Little BIG chats
Little books to help kids unpack BIG topics
Consent
Introducing consent and body boundaries
by Jayneen Sanders Illustrated by Cherie Zamazing

Little BIG chats
Little books to help kids unpack BIG topics
Secrets and Surprises
Learning the difference between secrets and surprises
by Jayneen Sanders Illustrated by Cherie Zamazing

Little BIG chats
Little books to help kids unpack BIG topics
Private Parts are Private
Learning private parts are private and what to do if touched inappropriately
by Jayneen Sanders Illustrated by Cherie Zamazing

Little BIG chats
Little books to help kids unpack BIG topics
My Safety Network
Introducing a Safety Network (3 to 5 trusted adults a child can go to if they feel unsafe)
by Jayneen Sanders Illustrated by Cherie Zamazing

Little BIG chats
Little books to help kids unpack BIG topics
My Early Warning Signs
Exploring Early Warning Signs and what to do if a child experiences these signs
by Jayneen Sanders Illustrated by Cherie Zamazing

Little BIG chats
Little books to help kids unpack BIG topics
Families
Celebrating diversity in families
by Jayneen Sanders Illustrated by Cherie Zamazing

Little BIG chats
Little books to help kids unpack BIG topics
I Always Try
Developing a growth mindset of resilience and persistence
by Jayneen Sanders Illustrated by Cherie Zamazing

Little BIG chats
Little books to help kids unpack BIG topics
Feelings
Understanding different feelings and emotions
by Jayneen Sanders Illustrated by Cherie Zamazing

Little BIG chats
Little books to help kids unpack BIG topics
Everyone is Equal
Introducing the importance of gender equality and diversity
by Jayneen Sanders Illustrated by Cherie Zamazing

Little BIG chats
Little books to help kids unpack BIG topics
Empathy
Exploring the meaning of empathy and kindness
by Jayneen Sanders Illustrated by Cherie Zamazing

Little BIG chats
Little books to help kids unpack BIG topics
Mindfulness
Exploring the importance of mindfulness and learning calming skills
by Jayneen Sanders Illustrated by Cherie Zamazing

Little BIG chats
Little books to help kids unpack BIG topics
Around the World
Celebrating racial equality and diversity
by Jayneen Sanders Illustrated by Cherie Zamazing

www.ingramcontent.com/pod-product-compliance
Lightning Source LLC
Chambersburg PA
CBHW040002040426
42337CB00032B/5201